TAKING
TECHNOLOGY
TO MARKET

Six Stages to Success

TAKING TECHNOLOGY TO MARKET

Six Stages to Success

ROGER E. LEVIEN, PH.D.

CRISP PUBLICATIONS

Editor-in-Chief: *William F. Christopher*

Managing Editor: *Kathleen Barcos*

Editor: *Regina Preciado*

Cover Design: *Kathleen Barcos*

Cover Production: *Russell Leong Design*

Book Design & Production: *London Road Design*

Printer: *Bawden Printing*

Library of Congress Card Catalog Number 97-66242

ISBN 1-56052-439-1

PREFACE

Technological innovation occurs more rapidly now than ever before and its pace continues to increase. As a result, the stock of technology available to meet human needs is expanding at a growing rate. Regrettably, the capacity to translate technological potential into products and services that can both satisfy customers and reward investors is not expanding correspondingly. Despite the enthusiasm and energy of their inventors, many technologies fail to reach the market or fail quickly when they reach there. And that occurs whether the inventor worked alone in his garage or had the resources of an existing business to draw upon. A principal reason for the lack of market success is the failure to recognize that creating a successful business to take a technology to market is as challenging and demanding of creative effort as the invention of the technology itself. Consequently, many of the business activities required to reach market are performed hastily, poorly, or not at all; and people with the creative skills and experience required to perform them well are not engaged. The purpose of this book is to provide inventors of new technologies with a roadmap for taking technology to market that will help them avoid those errors and, therefore, deliver products or services that will satisfy customers' needs while rewarding inventors and their investors.

The six-stage process for taking technology to market that this book describes is my distillation and organization of recommendations and practices from many sources.

Some of them are listed in the section entitled "Further Reading" at the end of the book. But many ideas have come from my own and my associates' experience at Xerox and from the shared experiences of colleagues at other organizations. I would be lax if I did not acknowledge them as sources or helpful critics of the ideas that I have gathered and integrated in this document.

For several years at Xerox I was privileged to lead Technology and Market Development (TMD), an organization within Corporate Research and Development, that was the test bed both for new business development and for best practices for such development within the context of a large corporation. The experience of TMD and its lessons—both positive and negative—have shaped the recommended practices in this book. I am grateful to my colleagues in TMD for their vigorous engagement in our joint efforts to build businesses and learn from the experience. They are: Joseph Daniele, Edward Ernst, Andy Garman, John Knights and Bettie Steiger. Mark Myers, the Senior Vice President of Corporate Research and Technology, worked hard to provide an environment in which technology could move rapidly and profitably to market.

During that same time, I was fortunate to participate in the Commercialization Roundtable, an informal group of colleagues who met several times a year for a number of years to discuss our common efforts to succeed in the challenging task of creating new businesses within large corporations. By sharing openly our successes and failures, we all benefited; by trying to distill those experiences into

best practices, we all learned. I was a primary beneficiary
and the process proposed in this book incorporates what
I learned. My fellow travelers (with their organizations
at that time) on that voyage of discovery were: Sharon
Arthur of IBM, Robert Burton of Motorola, Joe Cote of
GTE, Pat Foley of DuPont, Fernand Kaufman of Dow
Chemical, Jeanne Lyons of Digital, Jay Paap of the Data
and Strategies Group, Merlin Schulze of MCC, Dick Scott
of GTE, and Bettie Steiger of Xerox. I owe them a large
debt of gratitude, but they are not to blame for any misin-
terpretations or omissions in my distillation of our shared
experiences.

Three colleagues read the manscript as a whole
and made many helpful suggestions, most of which I
have incorporated. They are: Merlin Schulze of MDS
Associates, Ken Rind of Oxford Partners, and Wayland
Hicks of Indigo. I am deeply grateful to them for sharing
the benefits of their experience with new business
development.

William Christopher, the editor of this series, bears
ultimate responsiblity for the existence of this book.
Without his initiative, encouragement and patient support,
I would probably neither have started nor finished this
manuscript. I am happy he persisted; he has my warm
thanks.

My wife, Carla, accepted my evening and weekend
disappearances into the study with her usual good grace.
In this, as in so many other activities, she has been my
steadfast support. I am delighted to be able to acknowledge her strong role in our partnership.

CONTENTS

CONTENTS

I.

Six Stages to Success

CHALLENGE
*Taking a technology from the
laboratory or garage to success in the marketplace.*

S O YOU'VE FOUND A new technology that you think
will meet important customer needs; that will do so
better than anything else available; and that can be
produced and sold at a profit. *Congratulations!* You've come
a long way. *Sorry!* You still have a long way to go.

Your technology idea may be the essential seed from
which a profitable new business will grow. But it will need
lots of nourishment and support. It will have to be supplemented by many more creative ideas before it can return
a profit for you and the financial backers. And those ideas
will be in fields distant from technology–finance, manufacturing, marketing, and sales–where you may have very little knowledge and no experience. In fact, the technology
idea represents just the first of many creative ideas required
to deliver value to the customer who will be willing to pay
for it.

This book lays out a six-stage path that technology
ideas–whether developed in a laboratory of an existing

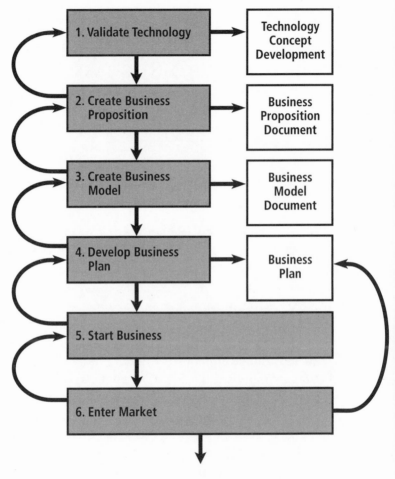

Figure 1. Six stages to the market

corporation or hatched in a lone inventor's garage—can take to market. It describes the challenges you will face at each stage. And it suggests ways to analyze and overcome each of them. If you can surmount the challenges, you have a good chance of market success and profit. Should one of them prove insurmountable, however; well, you and your colleagues can return to the laboratory or garage and try again; this time with an enhanced appreciation of the requirements for success.

Before we get down to specifics in the following chapters, let's survey the six stages from technology to market, as shown in Figure 1, and the challenges faced at each stage.

The first four stages develop the business idea, starting with the technology concept and culminating in the business plan, possibly returning one or more times to revise the technology as you learn more about the business opportunity.

STAGE 1. TECHNOLOGY IDEA

Challenge: *Establishing that the technology is ready, advantaged and protected.*

STAGE 2. BUSINESS PROPOSITION

Challenge: *Defining a realistic business concept and value proposition.*

STAGE 3. BUSINESS MODEL

Challenge: *Designing the value chain: which functions will be performed internally and which externally? Establishing a profitable financial model.*

STAGE 4. BUSINESS PLAN

> Challenge: *Describing the business opportunity.*
> *Specifying the action plan. Determining*
> *the resource requirements and the*
> *financial returns.*

The result of each of the first four stages is captured in a document, which should be reviewed by experienced and critical advisors. It costs much less to discover mistakes through early critical review than through later hard experience—even though that is not always possible. The business plan you prepare during the fourth stage will incorporate all that you have learned in the preceding stages, adding the information that is required to complete a blueprint for the business. You will use this blueprint to sell your idea to those whose good will, authorization, participation, or cash is required to enable your business to start up.

Assuming that the business plan has generated support and resources, in the last two stages the business idea is turned into reality: first, by creating the business organization, and then, by launching the initial product into the marketplace. The results are no longer documents, but actions and their effects: all the elements of a business working together; a product successfully delivered to and received by its intended consumers.

STAGE 5. BUSINESS START-UP

> Challenge: *Establishing the business and adapting*
> *the plan to reality.*

Stage 6. Market Entry

Challenge: *Taking the offering to market and meeting the ultimate challenge: satisfying real customers in the face of competition and making a profit (and sometimes revising the Business Plan based on hard experience).*

It is not necessary to finish one stage before *beginning* another. Several stages can proceed in parallel. In fact, it may be best to carry on several steps in parallel, since that may reveal problems early and avoid surprises. It is essential, however, that they *finish* in order. In other words, you cannot complete the second stage before the first, because it must build upon the conclusions of the first; similarly, the third stage completion must await finishing the second. And so on to the sixth. Even though a stage is completed, it may be necessary to return to it to make changes suggested by a later stage.

If you can surmount each of the challenges, you stand a reasonable chance of success in the market. But don't forget, just as you are struggling to bring your technology idea to market, so are others. If you have identified an attractive market, the chances are good that someone else will be addressing that same market, perhaps with different technology. Whether you succeed depends, therefore, not only on how well you traverse these six stages, but on how the resultant business compares—in the marketplace—with your competitors' endeavors. And sadly for technologists, that competition is not always—or even usually—won by the best technology. Rather, the winner is the one who most successfully executes the entire business, taking advantage of market timing, pricing, advertising, partnerships, name and reputation, and any other source of advantage that the competitor can find. Probably it will be creative business ideas, not the original technology idea, that will prove crucial to your market success. (See the *Case in Point,* below.)

Case in Point: The xerographic plain paper copier, one of the most successful technology innovations of this century, might have met early failure had it not been for a critical business idea. When the Xerox 914, the first xerographic copier, was about to be introduced in 1959, market studies suggested that customers would hesitate to pay the price to buy a plain paper copier, which was substantially more expensive than the chemical and coated paper copiers it would be seen as replacing. Marketing then suggested that the copier be leased for a modest monthly rental fee ($95) and after a free allowance (2,000 copies), all subsequent copies be paid for at 3.5 cents each. Because a mechanical counter was used to keep track of the number of copies made, this was called the "click charge." The low rental fee made it easy for companies to try the new technology; the click charge—an operating and not a capital charge—became the source of great profits as each company's employees discovered the value of the copier and rapidly increased its use.

II.

THE TECHNOLOGY IDEA

CHALLENGE

*Establishing that the technology is
ready, advantaged, and protectable.*

Y OU ARE BEGINNING THIS quest because a laboratory, garage or office has given birth to a technology idea that you and others familiar with it believe can be the basis for a profitable business. Your first step must be to assure yourself and your associates that the technology satisfies the minimum requirements to become the basis for a business. There are three such requirements:

- **Readiness:** The technology is ready if it is possible to develop a product or service from it using standard engineering practice—without the need for further basic invention.

- **Advantage:** The technology is advantaged if it enables development of a product or service that can hold its own against likely competitors at the time of its market entry. A sufficient number of customers must be expected to prefer it to its competitors—at its likely price—to hold promise of a profitable business.

- **Protectability:** The technology is protectable if, through some combination of patents, copyrights, and trade secrets, you can prevent competitors from copying it. Or, alternately, with early market entry and rapid evolution, the technology can sustain advantage against competitive followers.

Figure 2 shows the flow of analyses and decisions that must be completed at this stage.

Readiness

The first decision—*readiness*—depends on the information available for the specific technology and the ease of testing its status. To ensure that the judgment is as useful as possible, you should consult with experts who have direct experience in turning your kind of technology into products (or services).

- An electronic technology can be shown to operate in a computer simulation, a breadboard mock-up, a prototype, or a full-scale working model. If one or more of those demonstrations establishes that the technology achieves what is claimed, that it is robust enough to do so under a range of reasonable variations of its environment, and that there are no fundamental impediments to scaling up the technology for manufacturing and use then you can pronounce the technology ready.

- Large-scale hardware technology is not always demonstrable in the laboratory. In the chemical industry, for example, laboratory demonstrations

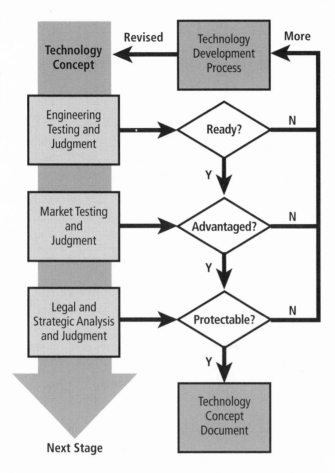

*Figure 2.   Establishing that the technology is ready,
advantaged and protectable*

may be followed by several stages of scale-up before
the technology is approved for plant-scale production.
Thus, readiness may be more difficult and expensive

to judge in some technologies, such as chemical processing, than in others, such as software.

- Some technologies, especially those with a substantial software component, may actually be developed in association with an end-user and can, therefore, establish their validity through the demonstration of a working prototype performing useful functions for a customer. In such cases, the readiness judgment is easily made.

You will have an understandable desire, as will the business people who want to take your technology to market, to move forward as quickly as possible. To do so, you will be tempted to take an optimistic view of the readiness of the technology. Be warned: Considerable hard experience demonstrates that this unrealistic approach leads to problems at a later stage, which will take longer and cost more to overcome than a first-stage effort to achieve true readiness. In rapidly moving fields, it is often better to spend heavily and solve technical problems quickly to enable market entry ahead of competition.

Advantage

The second decision—*advantage*—is a judgment based on an initial appreciation of customer requirements and competitive alternatives. In the easiest case, both of these are well-known and understood. For many advanced technology ideas, however, you will find neither established customer requirements nor existing competitors. Furthermore, at this stage you will have only an initial idea of the product or service that you will bring to market; you will develop that during the next stage. For now you can best work with your initial broad concepts and use the information you gain to guide refinement at the next stage.

- You can establish customer requirements through engagement of prospective customers under proper confidential disclosure agreements. Interview them, show them concept drawings or story boards, engage them in simulations of use, or use them as "guinea pigs" for early prototypes. Alternately, in an existing market, well-established customer requirements for higher performance at lower cost (for example, in PC speed and memory) may serve as an adequate guide to determining the prospective advantage of a new technology.

- Will a sufficient number of customers prefer the cost/performance of products enabled by the new technology to competitors and substitutes, including those using the current technology? In many cases, the primary competitor to a new technology will be the existing technology. Even if the current product is inferior to a new technology, customer satisfaction and unwillingness to incur the costs of a switch, such as training and process redesign, may protect it. For example, many customers may be unwilling to pay much more for the improved picture quality of high-definition television, despite the technological advances that it represents. A substantial cost-performance advantage may be required to displace an entrenched competitor. The requirement can be as much as 2 to 3 times improvement; 20% is generally insufficient to overcome the costs in time and effort of switching.

- Evaluate your competitors' performance through benchmarking of their current performance *and extrapolating their anticipated performance at the date your products or services enter the market.* By doing this conscientiously, you will avoid the common mistake of assuming that the competition will stand still while you bring your new technology to market. You have no excuse for not gaining a deep understanding of the competitive technologies and their probable evolution.

The judgment you must make at this stage may be the most difficult one of the entire process of moving to market. Every technology innovator believes that his or her technology will satisfy customer needs better than all substitutes. But when market investigation suggests otherwise, it can be difficult to distinguish natural enthusiasm from the brilliant insight of the pioneer who perceives a latent need that will lead to an entirely new market. Chester Carlson, who saw the need for plain paper copying in the mid-1930s, could not get support from any large corporation. It was only the complementary foresight of Joseph Wilson, the president of a small photographic paper company that eventually became Xerox, that enabled the technology to reach market, twenty-five years later in 1959!

Protectability

The third decision–*protectability*–is also a matter
of judgment and degree. Few ideas are completely protectable, because human ingenuity and technological
potential are so great that–given time–almost all protected
technologies can be circumvented. In fact, the virtue of
intellectual property protection, through patents, copyrights, and trade secrets, is the time it buys, even if it is
not the full term of the patent or copyright. During the
protected time you have a legal monopoly for the use of
your technology. So, where protection is possible, it would
be foolhardy not to take advantage of it.

- Intellectual property protection is both a legal and a
  strategic matter. At a minimum, the principal features
  of the technology idea should be patented and, where
  appropriate, such as for software, copyrighted. (Of
  course, the first question is whether someone else got
  there first. A patent search should reveal prior patents
  that might affect your technology.) Apply for patents
  in those countries where a reasonable chance exists
  that a large enough market will develop. In addition,
  you should develop a strategy to extend the patents
  and their claims so as to establish a blocking position
  against likely alternative technology approaches.

- If the technology is not patentable, you may still be
  able to protect it through trade secrets; indeed, this
  may be preferable in situations where revealing the
  technology in a patent may open it for surreptitious
  replication or circumvention by a competitor. Your

best protection, especially in rapidly changing fields of technology, may be achieved through early entry into the market and rapid evolution of the technology on the basis of market experience so as to keep one generation ahead of competitors.

If you find that someone else's protected technology is essential to your product or service idea, you will need to negotiate a license to use that technology. That will probably entail payment of a royalty (which can be a percentage of revenues, a fixed amount, or even equity in your company). Whatever form it takes, you must account for it in the financial model developed in the third stage.

Technology Concept Document

If your judgment is negative on any one of the three issues, the technology must go back to its source for further development to overcome the identified deficiency. But, if all three judgments are favorable, you and the technology are ready to move on to the next stage.

Before doing so, prepare a *Technology Concept Document* summarizing your decisions. Your report should comprise five sections:

- Technology Concept Description

- Readiness

- Advantage

- Protectability

- Conclusion and Critical Assumptions

Each section should summarize the information you used in making your positive judgments. Conclude with the critical assumptions about the technology that support your positive decision. Identify these assumptions specifically so that they can be re-examined as additional information becomes available. Should one of the critical assumptions be shown to be false or to need significant modification, the technology concept or business idea based on it needs to be re-examined.

III.

THE BUSINESS PROPOSITION

CHALLENGE
*Defining a realistic business concept
and value proposition.*

AFTER VERIFYING THAT THE technology idea has potential value, your next step is to consider two basic business questions, whose answers define the business proposition.

- What will be offered, to whom, and through which channels?

- Why and how will it be paid for?

The answer to the first question defines the *business concept*. The answer to the second establishes the *value proposition*.

How can you answer these questions? First, remember that these are design questions. Creativity plays an essential role. There are no predetermined answers. No established analytical process will compute the solutions. Sometimes the answers will seem obvious and perhaps they will prove to be. But it is best to let the obvious answer fight for dominance over alternatives. Often enough, open-minded thought will reveal a less obvious possibility that will open new opportunities for customer value and marketplace advantage.

Business Concept

What *offerings*—products or services—will be brought to market? To which *market segment*—group of customers sharing some distinguishing property—will they be offered?

MARKET SEGMENTS

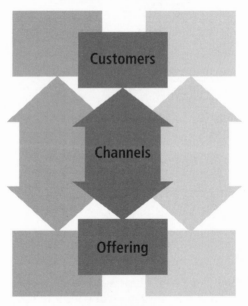

BUSINESS

Figure 3. A business concept—offerings to segments through channels

Through which *channels*—organizations for distribution and sales—will the product be offered? Your answers to these three questions will give you a high level design of the business vehicle that will deliver the technology's value to its users. The three elements—offerings, market segments, channels—describe your business concept. A *business concept* is shown schematically in Figure 3.

Offerings

What form or forms will the technology take in the market? To see how wide the range of possible forms can be, let's consider an example. Suppose you have invented a technology that combines hardware and software to deliver high-quality, two-way video conferencing to two or more users on a network. What are some of the possible offerings derived from that technology?

- The hardware and software could be sold together.

- The software could be sold alone to run on hardware others provided.

- The hardware and software could be offered in a package with installation and training services.

- The hardware and software could be leased to users.

- A video conferencing service could be provided for a charge based on time, distance, and number of users.

- The service could be delivered through arrangements with local and long-distance telephone companies.

Each of these offerings is a different way of delivering the technology's value to its users. They deliver similar operational values to the end user, but they differ substantially in the subsidiary requirements that the user's organization must satisfy. And they challenge the business in different ways, requiring different skills, investments, channels, and management structures, and resulting in different costs of ownership.

The exact choice of offering in any situation will depend upon the nature of the existing market. What are the competitive offerings? Do customers have obvious preferences? Do you see an unmet need in the market for a new form of delivery? Will it be easier to reach customers or for them to pay in a certain form? You need to address these questions carefully, applying what you learned in the first stage, and using similar approaches to test the ideas as they evolve. The choice of an offering is a crucial step to success—or failure.

Market Segments

As you address the question of what to offer, you will also have to answer the question: to whom? For most technology innovations, the world of potential customers is not a homogeneous mob with identical needs. Your prospective customers will differ in their performance requirements, their ability to pay, and in their willingness to try something new. It is, therefore, generally desirable to identify one or a small number of subgroups within the market whose needs, financial resources and capacity for innovation are best suited to the offering you are conceiving. Those become your target market segments.

The challenge at this stage is to avoid two opposing dangers. The first danger is being too inclusive. If you try to meet the needs of too broad a range of customers, the offering's specifications will become a compromise for most users. Furthermore, the costs of reaching too many customers may become excessive. The second, and opposite, danger is narrow exclusivity. You don't want to optimize the offering for a group of customers that is too small for financial success.

Market segmentation in new markets is an art form. If your technology meets previously latent needs and opens entirely new markets, you can reason by analogy with other related markets or by estimating what customer qualities are likely to lead to different responses to the technology. Test these hypotheses through direct engagement with potential customers in focus groups, demonstrations, simulations, or other situations intended to show them a prospective offering and to obtain their reaction to its qualities. When drawing conclusion from such tests, take into account the participants' difficulty in accurately anticipating their needs for entirely new products.

In contrast, market segmentation in well-established markets is a common activity, with many experienced practitioners. Enlist the support of marketing specialists familiar with your target market to help at this stage.

Channels

The channel of distribution is the mechanism through which your offering is brought to the attention of its prospective customers, sold to them, delivered to them and (when necessary) serviced. The channel also often sets final sales prices and collects revenues from the customer.

Channels fall into two major categories: direct and indirect. A direct channel is managed by the company that developed the offering. An indirect channel is managed by a separate company. For example, IBM sells its mainframe computers through a sales force that it employs and manages, but distributes its personal computers through dealers owned by other corporations.

Channel structure differs among industries, markets, and even customers. Often a customer can obtain the same kind of product through several different types of channels. For example, you can buy personal computers directly from the manufacturer, through dealers, by mail order, by phone order, or as part of complex systems designed, delivered, and supported by custom system designer/integrators. Which channels customers choose depends upon their needs, resources, and tastes. Their choices are also strongly affected by experience with the quality of service provided by each channel.

For some offerings based on new technologies, a direct channel may be required. When you control the channel, you can ensure the full attention of the sales force, even in the face of problems with the offering. You can exercise tight control over the administration of the channel's resources, directing them to the most promising customers you can identify through all the information you have available. You can also more closely control pricing and the quality of customer service. And information about customers and competitors gathered by a direct sales force feeds more directly into the strategy and tactics of the business.

For other innovative technologies, an indirect channel may be essential. Where an existing channel efficiently reaches your target market segment, with high satisfaction, you may have little choice but to use it. For example, almost all personal computer printers (laser and ink jet) are sold through computer and office equipment dealers. Attempting to sell a competitive printer product without gaining access to dealer "shelf space" would be extremely difficult. But with such access, the channel can establish contact with a large number of customers far more quickly than a newly created direct channel can.

In some cases you may want to use multiple channels, selecting different channels to reach different customer segments.

The Concept

You have now defined the three basic elements of your business concept:

- *The Offering:* the product or service you intend to deliver

- *Market Segments:* the specific groups of customers to whom you will deliver it

- *The Channel:* the means by which the offering will reach the customers and they will pay for it

Complements and Substitutes

In order for your business concept to succeed when it enters the market, it must establish its position with regard to other offerings in that market. These fall into two categories: complements and substitutes. (These ideas are introduced and developed as a basis for strategic thinking in References 5a and 5b.)

An offering is a *complement* to yours if it increases the value of your product to the consumer. For example, software is the essential complement to computer hardware. Neither has much value to the customer without the other. In specific instances, even tighter linkages have occurred. The IBM PC's success was tightly linked to the popularity of Lotus 1-2-3, which in turn could not have succeeded without the PC. The Apple Macintosh found its first widespread success in desktop publishing, where its complements were Aldus Pagemaker composition software, Adobe Postscript page description language and the laser printer. More recently, the World Wide Web network architecture has grown at a spectacular pace because of the ease of use and attractiveness of the Mosaic browser and its descendants.

An offering is a *substitute* for yours if it decreases the value of your product to the consumer. For example, Microsoft's Excel is a substitute for Lotus 1-2-3. Its existence establishes a competitive environment in which the value of each is less than it would be in a situation when only one is available. Substitutes need not employ similar technology. For example, a paper spreadsheet and desk calculator together form a substitute for a computer and Excel or Lotus 1-2-3. For a new technology, the most important substitute may be the way the function is performed currently.

You should identify, as completely as possible, your offering's complements and its substitutes. Where complements are critical to your success, you must include their stimulation in your concept and plans. For the substitutes, you should prepare responses and understand how to increase your value to your chosen customers in comparison.

Supplies

To bring your offering to market, you will in turn be the customer for the offerings of others. An offering is a supply to you if it is required to produce your product or service. The supply can be labor, materials, capital equipment, or loans of cash. The value of these supplies will determine the cost of your offering. Where they are offered in a highly competitive market, you can be reasonably confident that you can retain all the additional value you add in your offering. However, if one or more of your critical supplies is controlled by a single supplier or is in short supply, and you can find no substitutes at the same price, you may be forced to share your value added with that supplier. For example, the 1994 baseball strike was a negotiation between suppliers of a service in short supply (major-league baseball players) and team owners whose offering, (major-league baseball) required their services, over the division of the value delivered by the teams to their customers.

In meeting your needs, your suppliers' offerings have substitutes and complements as well. The substitutes reduce the value of the supplies to you, because you can obtain your needs elsewhere; while the complements increase the value of the supplies.

Value Net

Figure 4 illustrates the relationships among your customer, your offering, its supplies, substitutes and complements. This is different from a related figure

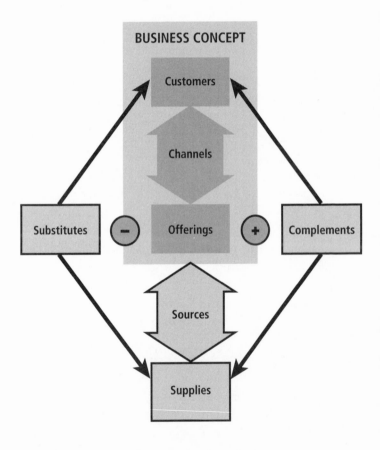

Figure 4.   The value net for a business concept

in References 5a and 5b, but better suits our purposes. Before proceeding to the next step, you should draw such a diagram specifically for your business concept, paying careful attention to your substitutes and complements. References 5a and 5b also show how this diagram can be used to think through your business strategy.

Value Proposition

You must also address two fundamental financial questions: What *value* will be delivered to the customer? What *price* will the customer pay for it? Your answers will help to determine whether the business can earn enough to cover its expenses and return a profit to its investors. The *value-price pairing* establishes the basic *value proposition*.

Value

The most fundamental question you must answer about your proposed business is: *Why will customers buy what is being offered?* What aspect of their lives will be improved if they buy your product or service compared with their present state or the result of buying one of the substitutes? You must be specific. It is not enough to say they will be more productive or happier or better fed. You should be able to explain: "They'll be more productive because they will be able to double the number of tasks they can accomplish in a day." Or: "They'll be happier because they'll have twice the selection of high quality entertainment."

Then you should ask: how much will that improved state be worth to the customers? Would it be worth twice what they are currently spending? Or would it be worth as much as a theater ticket? Rough estimates are enough to begin with. These values will differ among individual customers but those in your target market segments should be similar enough to be treated as one.

Price

Turning the question around, you should now ask: *what will the business have to charge for its offerings to return a profit that will justify the investment?* At this first stage, your answer will have to be an approximation, which you will refine as you move on to subsequent stages. For now you need only the most basic answers.

If the required price is substantially higher than the worth of the offering to the prospective customers, the business is not viable and must be redefined. You must find a way to deliver value of greater worth, or to reduce the necessary price, or both, if the business is to be worth starting.

If, however, the required price is comfortably below the worth of the offering to a large enough number of customers, the business has passed its second hurdle: the basic business proposition is reasonable.

Business Proposition

To capture the results of this second stage, prepare your Business Proposition. It should comprise three sections:

- Business Concept
  - Offerings

- ○ Market Segments
- ○ Channels
- ○ Value Net
- Value Proposition
  - ○ Value
  - ○ Price
- Conclusion and Critical Assumptions

Each section should summarize the choices made and the reasons for them. The concluding section should contain the critical assumptions about each element of the business proposition. As with the technology assumptions, these will have to be continually checked as the business develops so as to ensure that the basis for the business has not significantly changed.

IV.

THE BUSINESS MODEL

CHALLENGE
*Designing the value chain: which functions will be
performed internally and which externally?
Establishing a profitable financial model.*

YOU NOW HAVE DESIGNED a customer's eye view of your business: what it offers, through what channels, to whom and for how much. But the business itself remains a black box. Inside the box are all the things that must be done to produce and deliver the offerings the customers want. That black box also comprises the financial engine that receives revenues, covers expenses, and—with good design and management—produces a profit. In this stage, your challenge is to define what goes on inside that black box and to show how—after start-up—its operations will be profitable. Two questions must be answered:

1. Which functions will the business perform and which will it contract out?

2. How will the revenues be allocated among expenses and profit?

The answer to the first question determines the *value chain* for your business. The answer to the second question defines the target *financial model.*

Although creativity helps in establishing the answers to these questions, experience and guidelines will prove useful as well. You must pay attention to the lessons of other businesses at this stage. Otherwise, it is all too easy to let wishful thinking gain the upper hand, leading to unrealistically optimistic financial models. Using comparable businesses as models is the best reality check known.

Value Chain

Michael Porter's classic text on business strategy, *Competitive Advantage,* brought to wide attention and use the idea of the value chain for a business. (See Reference 13.) The value chain shown in Figure 5 represents all the activities that must be performed, more or less in order, to bring an offering to market. (This is slightly different from Porter's representation, but better fits our needs.)

Research and Development (Product Development)

Research and development in some form led to the ready, advantaged and protected technology that you want to take to market. In the ongoing business, R&D will be responsible for the major innovations, for all the invention and engineering required to prepare the first product offering for manufacturing, and for producing the continuing stream of improved, variant, and new products necessary to sustain the business. It must do so in

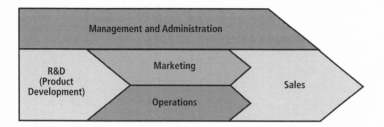

Figure 5. The value chain

close communication with marketing and with manufacturing operations. Although a service business may not have a separately defined R&D (or Product Development) department, conceptually an identical need exists for the design of the offering. Service R&D is often done more intuitively than product R&D.

Marketing

Marketing is responsible for the dialog between the business and its customers. (For several good books on marketing strategy for start-ups, see References 6, 11, 12a, 12b.) At the beginning, marketing focuses on identifying the customers to be served (the target market segments) and their needs (customer requirements). It should work closely with research and development to translate those requirements into product specifications, and make sure that the identified needs are met.

Once the product has been specified and developed, marketing is responsible for communicating to the marketplace the availability, features and advantages of the offering. This will be through public relations activities such as news releases, press conferences, and press or analyst tours; as well as through traditional advertising, booths at trade shows, and Internet home pages. It must also provide substantial assistance to the sales function through the provision of brochures, demonstration units, videotapes, and other collaterals that explain the offering's advantages and justifications for its purchase.

Operations

Operations is a composite term that covers all steps from purchasing components through manufacturing to shipment to the customer, and billing and customer support. Purchasing and manufacturing, together with careful design, are responsible for the quality, timeliness and cost of the product. In fast moving competitive markets, they share with product development the critical responsibility for rapid time to market. In almost all cases, their effective performance will be essential to the success of your hardware product. (They are, of course, less critical in the case of software products and meaningless in the delivery of a service.) The logistics system that takes the product from manufacturing through delivery to the customer can also be a source of advantage or disadvantage. By keeping inventories of the product and its spare parts to a minimum, by getting the product to the customer on time and quickly, and by seeing that the customer receives a fully functional product, the logistics function can benefit your business. Too often, however, the logistic function delivers the opposite—large inventories, delayed or missed deliveries, and non-functional products—which adversely affects the business. Customer support, billing and collection can all be sources of dissatisfaction to customers if not performed well; if performed satisfactorily, customers tend to take these functions for granted.

Sales

Sales, in contrast with marketing, is concerned with customers as individuals, not as categories. Its task is to complete the transaction that delivers value to the customer in exchange for a payment. Normally, the sales function requires a sales force whose task is to convince the customer that the product will satisfy the customer's requirements better than the alternatives–including not buying anything. Increasingly, sales of familiar and relatively inexpensive products are being made without an end-customer sales force, using instead catalogs, superstores, on-line catalogs, and other sales media. However, when products are distinctive, unlike anything currently on the market, or expensive, a human sales force is likely to be essential.

Management and Administration

The role of management is difficult to specify briefly, but its effects are always evident. It is the difference between the business' success and failure. Management sets the direction of the business, acquires and allocates resources, establishes priorities, represents the business to its constituencies, selects and motivates people and establishes the business' culture. It is the one function that cannot be outsourced. Not sufficient in itself to make up for deficiencies in the offering, marketing, or sales, it is necessary to mobilize, coordinate, and monitor the functions to achieve their full success. Establishing the business' vision and goals, setting short-term objectives, assessing progress, and making necessary changes in plans, personnel, and resources are critical functions of management. And it is management that must take primary responsibility for the financial assets of the business, both their acquisition and their productive use.

The administrative function has the day-to-day oversight and operational responsibilities for the financial, human, physical and other assets of the business.

Internal or External?

These five functions appear in the value-added chain of any business. In designing your business, you must decide which functions your business should perform itself and which it should contract for from suppliers or partners. Two principles should guide this choice:

1. *A function should be carried out internally if and only if it cannot be performed better by someone else.*

    Think of each function as a potential source of competitive advantage—or disadvantage. If manufacturing internally is slower and more expensive than using a job shop, which might be able to draw on a larger capital investment, longer experience, better trained staff, and higher volumes to amortize overhead, then internal manufacturing is potentially giving cost and time advantages to a competitor. On the other hand, if your technology incorporates proprietary and advantaged manufacturing processes, then keeping them internal may be critical.

2. *Those functions that are the source of competitive advantage for your business should be carried out under the business' complete control.*

The key to your business' success is the effective exploitation of its advantages, whether those lie in technology alone or include marketing, manufacturing, or sales as well. You can best accomplish this when you have complete control over those functions. Generally, that means they should be performed internally, under your management by your employees. Occasionally, it may be possible to execute an advantaged function through an external supplier, but only if the supplier is under your direct and tight control.

In the start-up stage of a business, it is particularly important to minimize unnecessary investment and staffing. It may also be difficult to find highly qualified functional management. Consequently, it makes sense to take these two principles very literally and limit the business to the absolute minimum of advantaged functions. Focus your attention on the few functions where you can add unique value and rely on contractors or partners for the others. When established companies adopt this approach, as some are currently, the result is called a "virtual corporation."

Financial Model

The financial model describes the flow of money through your business. That money is the fuel that enables your value chain to operate. The chain is primed with cash that you, your company, your bank, or your investors will provide. Each of them—even you—has alternative uses for that cash with a range of associated returns and risks. Investors put money into your business because they expect it to provide a better balance of risk and return than their other choices. It is your job to design a financial model that will fulfill that expectation.

Pro Forma Financial Model

The pro forma financial model shows you and your investors how the necessary returns will be produced once your value chain gets up to speed and the business moves beyond the initial start-up stage. In the early years, it will be "burning" cash in order to gain momentum; but after some reasonable time, the cash provided will have to be returned, with a premium sufficient to have justified the investment. That is the time when the pro forma financial

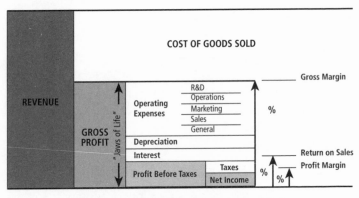

Figure 6. Pro forma financial model

model should apply. (Venture capital investors, in particular, may be less interested in the pro forma financial model than in the prospective market value of the business at the time of an Initial Public Offering. There is an association between those values, but future profitability and growth rate may be more significant determinants of market value.)

Figure 6 is a pro forma financial model for one year. Let us consider each element of that model. As you will see, each link in the value chain corresponds to one of the elements, although not all elements have a correspondence in the chain.

Revenue. The revenue of your ongoing business will come from several sources. The principal one will be the sale (or lease) of your offering. Additional revenues will come from supplies that the product uses (toner and photoreceptor cartridges for copiers and printers, for example) and for services, such as maintenance, training and operation. Since only you can forecast the revenues your business will be producing by the time it reaches the payback stage, we will deal in percentages. You should carry both absolute and percentage numbers along in your calculations. We will treat your total income or revenue as 100 percent. That is the money you have available (in the absence of additional investment) to run your business. How is it allocated among various elements? (Valuable sources of benchmark information about the structure of financial models can be found in References 1, 7, and 15.)

Cost of Goods Sold.   The first component to subtract
from revenue is "Cost of Goods Sold." This is what it has
cost to produce the offerings that resulted in your revenue.
Where you are selling products (not services), the cost of
goods sold is everything spent to produce the offering sold
to customers during the accounting year. It can be estimated as the number of units sold multiplied by the unit
manufacturing cost (it may also include some elements of
service cost and engineering expenses for ongoing product
improvement). In the case of services, the cost of goods
sold would be the salaries and expenses associated with
the delivery of the services.

Gross Profit—the "Jaws of Life."   The result of subtracting the cost of goods sold from revenue is "Gross Profit."
This is the real energizing force of your business. It is the
money that, on a sustaining basis, must cover all other
expenses of the business and leave a sufficient profit to
satisfy your investors. Without a large enough gross profit,
the business will die. To enlarge it, you must either *raise the
revenues* (by selling more or raising prices) or *lower the cost
of goods sold* (by redesigning or eliminating features, or by
increasing manufacturing efficiency). Think, therefore, of
this gap as the "jaws of life" of your business. Your goal is
to make this gap as large as possible.

Gross Margin.   Gross profit expressed as a percent of
revenue is "Gross Margin." Good product businesses will
have gross margins between 40 and 60 percent. Some
businesses exceed even the higher figure, especially successful software companies, which may reach 80–90%.

And some are much lower than the lowest figure, especially those that sell through indirect channels, in which the gross margin may be as low as 30 percent. Whatever, the percentage, it sets the bounds for your operating expenses as a percent of revenue. Clearly, the allocation of those expenses for a software company will be quite different from the allocation for a distributor of computers through mail order.

Operating Expenses.   Gross profit is applied to "Operating Expenses," "Depreciation," "Interest," and "Profit Before Taxes (PBT)." Operating expenses cover all those activities that are essential to the business: research and development, marketing, sales, operations, administration, and general management. Depreciation is the allocation to that accounting year of a portion of the costs of a capital investment with a multi-year life. Interest includes the payments to banks and other lenders for the use of their money. And PBT is the balance left after those expenses have been subtracted. Clearly, what can be devoted to operating expenses depends heavily upon the potential gross margin and required net profit. A business with 30 percent gross profit margin and a target PBT margin (called Return on Sales, or ROS) of 10 percent has only 20 percent of revenues to cover all operating expenses, depreciation, and interest.

Depreciation and Interest.   All else being equal, it is desirable for a business to minimize its capital investments. Nevertheless, every business does acquire capital assets to enhance the effectiveness and productivity of its human assets. Your business will do so also and you should make a good estimate of the amount and cost of the required assets. (You should also consider the option of outsourcing the capital-intensive functions or of leasing the facilities. By keeping your assets low, you will reduce the need for external financing.)

If you finance your business through loans, the interest paid on them will appear here. This number can vary quite widely and depends upon the financing model of the business. If it is funded entirely by loans, then the ability to make these payments without incurring further debt may be more important to your investors than the net profit.

You should also strive to minimize the loans you require to get your business started, although this advice is less clear cut. You may be better off borrowing enough to grow rapidly to the point where the loans can be easily paid off. In any event, the size of the loans required will depend less on your business model and more on your financial state. You may have sufficient equity capital to avoid loans and interest payments altogether.

Research and Development (Product Development).

The cost of product and process development is central to your technology-driven business. In the early years, it must cover the costs of taking the technology from the laboratory (or garage) and transforming it into a product for the market. That includes the design of the manufacturing process. Then it must transition to the mechanism for continued technology, product, and process innovation.

R&D is not only paid for by gross profit, it is critical to determining it. The engineering investment should increase the value of the product to the consumer, and therefore the price paid; it should also reduce the cost of the product. The result is that effective R&D is required to achieve and sustain good gross profits and margins. It pries open the business' "jaws of life."

R&D beyond start-up in a technology business is generally within the range of five to 15 percent of revenue; the former characterizing a mature business domain and the latter not unusual in very high-tech industries in rapidly changing markets.

Marketing. The marketing expense covers everything from product marketing, which interprets the customers' needs to the R&D function during product development, to marketing communication, which conveys the product's benefits to the customers. Effective marketing affects gross profit by increasing the volume of sales and the prices that customers are willing to pay.

Marketing expenses in a mature business might run from five to 15 percent of revenue and are highly dependent upon the sales model. An indirect sales model, for example, will often require substantial advertising expenditure–charged against marketing–to provide market pull for the product in the channel. A direct sales model, however, may not be able to afford as high an expenditure on advertising, because its sales costs will be higher.

Sales. If the sales function is carried out directly by sales personnel employed by your business, you'll pay the full cost of the sales function—sales salaries, equipment costs, and travel expenses—from gross profit. If it is done by a separate organization, an indirect channel, your costs will be lower, but you'll receive less revenue (by the amount of the dealer's discount), thus reducing gross profit and gross margin, assuming that cost of goods sold remains the same. A major advantage of indirect channels is that they cover most of the investments and expenses that would otherwise be required to establish a sales and distribution network, which can be a very big part of the total investment in a new business. Effective sales effort affects gross profit by increasing the volume of sales and the prices that customers are willing to pay.

Direct sales functions might cost 10 to 15 percent of sales, while indirect sales functions could be as little as five percent for the sales effort to the indirect channel and its management.

General Expenses.   All the other expenses of the business—rent, leased furniture and computers, general management, accounting, human resources management, books and subscriptions—fall in this category. Most of it adds little directly to gross profit and should be kept to an absolute minimum.

The value of general management, which includes the president/CEO and the chief financial officer, is harder to specify, but always evident. As noted earlier, it is the difference between success and failure. Especially in a new business, it pays to invest in experienced general management, who bring market and business knowledge that a start-up can rarely afford to gain on its own. A substantial component of their compensation, however, should be tied directly to the business' success.

General expenses should, in the absence of special circumstances, be 5–10 percent of revenue.

Profit Before Taxes (PBT). If the business is successful, the result of subtracting all the operating expenses, depreciation and interest from gross profit will be a positive number—the "Profit Before Taxes" or "PBT." If no realistic combination of revenue, cost of goods sold, depreciation, interest, and operating expenses produces positive PBT, then you probably do not have a business worth investment. You must go back to your business concept and revise it until you can find a realistic target business model that produces a positive PBT. Remember that we are looking for positive PBT at some time after an initial start-up period, which may last for several years, depending upon such factors as the business' basic profitability, its volume-dependent costs, and the achieved growth rate.

Note, however, that where a substantial fraction of the interest payment is for a short-term loan that will not be renewed, it may make sense to consider the appropriate measure of business viability, the profit before *interest* and taxes.

Remember that the purpose of considering this financial model is to examine the inherent viability of this business. You are asking: can I expect this business to produce a positive PBT under reasonable assumptions about gross profits and ongoing expenses after it reaches maturity? Prior to that time, however, you and the investors may decide to accept lower gross profits (by lowering prices) in order to increase sales volume, or higher operating expenses (by raising R&D, marketing or sales activities) in order to improve competitive position. Under those circumstances, the potential PBT is being "invested" in the business, with the expectation that it will produce faster growth and higher profits later.

Return on Sales. PBT as a percentage of revenues is "Return on Sales" (ROS). A reasonable target for many businesses is about 10 percent, but many special cases apply. And, in fact, from the investor's perspective, ROS is only a part of the equation. For what matters to investors is how much of their capital was required, for how long, to produce that return. Clearly, there is a big difference between two businesses that both have $10 million in revenue and $1 million in net profit (10 percent ROS), but where one business has $10 million in invested capital and the other has only $1 million. Thus, other measures of return take on importance.

Net Income (also Net Profit, Net Earnings) and Profit Margin. The result of subtracting estimated taxes from PBT is "Net Income" (also called "Net Profit" and "Net Earnings"). For actual performance purposes, this is the number that establishes what is left to reinvest in the company or pay out to shareholders each year. But because the tax rate is probably not a controllable variable in your tax planning, net income does not tell you much more than PBT about the viability of your business. Net income as a percentage of revenue is profit margin.

Returns on Equity and Assets.   If investors leave their
money in, in exchange for continuing ownership (equity)
in the business, then the annual "Return on Equity"
(ROE) is usually an important indicator for them. This
is calculated by dividing the net income by the total equity
invested by the shareholders. Because the amount of
equity (and debt) may not be known when you do your
initial financial model, an alternative ratio—the "Return
on Assets" (ROA)—can serve as a valuable indicator. It is
calculated by dividing the net income by the total assets of
the business; it, therefore, indicates profit as a percentage
of the funds provided both by shareholders and lenders.

***Figures of Merit for Investment: Net Present Value and
Internal Rate of Return.***   Your target financial model
enables you to understand how the various elements of
your business must work together—after the initial start-up
period—if it is to be financially successful. Unless you can
establish a credible model with adequate profitability,
your business is not viable. In addition to this test, your
investors will want it to pass more severe tests. They will
be interested in the stream of returns over a reasonable
time horizon in comparison with the investments required
to obtain them.

   To answer their questions, you will have to prepare,
as part of the Business Plan, a multi-year financial plan.
From that and from extrapolations beyond its horizon—in
the case of a Venture Capital funded start up, to the Initial
Public Offering—they will seek to identify the stream of
"Cash Flows" over time, initially negative and eventually
positive. From that stream, and an assumed interest rate,

you can calculate a "Net Present Value" (NPV) of the investment. If positive, the investment is good, though not necessarily as good as alternatives, which might have higher NPVs. Alternatively, you can find the interest rate at which the investment just reaches zero. That will be the "Internal Rate of Return" (IRR) of the investment. Detailed treatment of this subject can be found in texts on corporate finance. (See Reference 10, for example.)

Investors within a big corporation, the general management, who are considering investing in your business in comparison with other internal or external investment opportunities, may be most interested in the Internal Rate of Return. Taking into account all the investments over time, and the stream of net profits, what is the effective interest rate on the investment? How does that compare with the return on other investments? Not only must the investment in your business offer a better return than the alternatives, but it must also exceed the "cost of capital" of the corporation. Otherwise, it would be better for the corporation to borrow less or return equity to its investors.

Business Model

At this point you are prepared to describe your *Business Model*. The document should comprise the following sections:

- The Value Chain
  - Internal Functions
  - External Functions

- Financial Model
  - Gross Profit
  - Operating Expenses
  - Net Profit
  - Returns

- Conclusion and Critical Assumptions

In the first section, you should explain which functions of the value chain add competitive advantage and will be kept internal and why, and which functions can be performed by suppliers, allies or partners. In the second section, you should lay out the pro forma financial model, explaining how funds flow through the business and generate a positive return. It is especially important to justify each element of revenue, cost and expense by reference to actual data or by benchmarking comparable businesses. Finally, you should describe the critical assumptions that underlie and enable this positive outcome.

V.

THE BUSINESS PLAN

CHALLENGE
Describing the business opportunity.
Specifying the action plan.
Determining the resource requirements
and the financial returns.

B Y NOW, YOU HAVE established that you have a business concept with a reasonable chance of success—if it can be executed. You have described your offerings, customers, and channels and the value-price proposition. And you have spelled out the basic model for profitable business operations. You may have already received some support from corporate superiors or investors who are willing to bet on your idea. Your challenge now is to lay out in detail the steps to bring your idea to life. To do so, you will have to prepare a written plan for creating your business. This is also the document most likely to be used to raise the funds to get the business started.

What are the key topics to cover in your plan? First, you must explain as specifically and quantitatively as possible the market opportunity and how the offering derived from your technology will meet it better than the likely competition and other substitutes. Then, you should describe your action plan. What will be done? in what order? by whom? where? and what will it cost? What are the critical milestones? Finally, you will have to spell out the resource requirements. What people, facilities and equipment, and finances will be required to get started and operate until the business can become self-sustaining? Your goal will be to leave this stage with a Business Plan document that answers those questions.

Opportunity Description

At this stage, you must take your initial ideas about your offerings, the market segments you will serve, and your competition and make hard estimates about how your offerings will do during the business' first few years. These estimates are bound to be surrounded by a high degree of uncertainty, which you should try to express explicitly.

Markets and Customers

To begin with, you must put numerical estimates of size and growth over the next three to five years next to each of the market segments you targeted at the second stage. The availability of data and its accuracy will differ widely, depending upon the current state of development and analysis of the market and how close your offering is to existing offerings.

The most uncertain, but not uncommon, situation is when your technology enables the delivery of entirely new offerings to previously unserved or latent markets. There is unlikely to be any relevant market data, and that which exists is likely to have wide ranges of uncertainty. You will have to rely on your own information—perhaps a small survey of potential customers to establish need and interest—together with general data about market sizes to make a first order estimate of the likely market. The key assumptions that you make to generate these estimates should go on your list of critical assumptions that need to be validated as the development process continues.

The most certain, but not most common, situation is when your technology enables the delivery of an improved offering to previously served and analyzed markets. In that case, you can draw on existing sources of market data from consultants who specialize in that market or, sometimes, on public data provided by the government, professional societies or not-for-profit agencies.

Although it is not often done, you should show the range of uncertainty in each of your market numbers. You can do so in a variety of ways of increasing statistical sophistication. For initial business plan purposes, however, it is sufficient to estimate a base case and show low and high cases that represent the widest likely range of variation.

In addition to estimating the size and growth of each of your targeted market segments, you should carefully define the requirements of each group of customers that you intend to serve. Again, you may find little public data available to help. Instead, you should take the time to gather this information from potential customers yourself. Although customers cannot always articulate their latent needs, they may respond more positively when the potential offering is described to them. In any event, understanding your customers' requirements better than your competition is one of the best and most sustainable sources of competitive advantage.

Offerings vs. Competition

Having established that "large enough" markets exist with needs that you can meet, you should next describe the specific offerings that you intend to put on the market. Characterize the initial offering first by its performance in response to the identified customer needs, and then by its technology and cost. You can define subsequent offerings by their date of launch and their improvements in the established performance, technology or cost dimensions.

The most difficult, but most important, task here is to describe with equivalent care and detail the likely competitive offerings that will appear in the market at the same time as your offerings, and the other substitutes that your intended customer may have. Beware of the temptation to underestimate likely competitors (and substitutes) or to compare a future product with those currently in the market, ignoring their likely improvement. You should use your best efforts to characterize the competition accurately. Even if you are not aware of any competition, it is best to assume that there is another smart team capable of developing a similar product. Only in that way can you do everything possible to ensure that your offering is advantaged against the substitutes it will actually face at the time of its launch.

To conclude this topic, you should make an explicit comparison of your offerings against the anticipated competition and substitutes and identify the value you deliver and your sources of advantage. These should include both technological and other business advantages. As we noted earlier, it is not unusual for a technologically advantaged offering to lose in the marketplace. Such situations have occurred many times in the history of business and technology. Generally, this occurs because the winner has advantage in marketing or sales or, as has often happened, because it established itself first in the marketplace and no later competitor was "enough better" to displace it. Thus, if your competition is an entrenched product or service, you should plan to deliver substantial additional value and have very strong advantages to entice customers to change.

Growth Model

How fast will you be able to grow sales of your offerings in the markets that you have defined? Many factors are at work.

At one extreme, the market may be large but unserved, with substantial recognized needs, and a strong economic justification for buying the offering. In this situation, the growth may initially be limited only by the rate at which the offering can be produced, sold and delivered. Some, but relatively few, products have faced this happy condition. And, once opened, such markets will rapidly draw competitors.

At the other extreme, the market is large, but well-served, with relatively little need for improved performance and minimal economic justification for buying the new offering. In this situation, the growth may be limited—at best—to the natural replacement rate of the offering.

Still another possibility, which we discussed in Chapter 3, is that your offering will require complementary offerings from other businesses. For example, a new silverless film for the graphic arts industry requires adaptations to the industry's imagesetting devices for its use. In that case, the rate at which other businesses can adapt the imagesetters limits the rate of growth of the film business.

More typically for innovative technology, your offering may satisfy a real, but unrecognized, need in a potentially large market. You must convince each customer of the need and justification for purchase. Your salespeople will have to be missionaries and each sale will take a long time, not least because the customer may have no budget allocated for this kind of offering. In this situation, the growth is likely to be limited by the sales effort available.

Thus, to estimate your growth model, you will have to identify the limiting factor: is it production, replacement rate, availability of complements, sales effort or some other factor? From that, you can estimate the likely growth in sales over time, preferably showing base, high and low cases to account for the inherent uncertainty in any estimates.

Action Plan

To reach your growth potential, you need not only market demand and prospective offerings, but also the timely, effective execution of each of the functions in the value chain. At this stage in the planning, you need to spell out the tasks for each of the functions and the sequence in which they will be carried out.

Functional Plans

R&D has the primary responsibility to prepare your offerings for launch. What has to be done to develop the first product? How long is that likely to take? What are the intermediate milestones and checkpoints that enable progress to be monitored and proven?

Even though you may anticipate creating a small entrepreneurial organization with minimal bureaucracy, you should not make the mistake of assuming that means that R&D can operate without a formal process. Quite the contrary. So much rides on the successful completion of your product development, you should take special care to establish a careful schedule with well-specified checkpoints and milestones.

Moreover, you should anticipate that, despite best efforts, unexpected problems will delay your scheduled product launch beyond the predicted date. Unless you build some provisions into your plan to allow for that delay, you may run out of funds or expend marketing and sales effort prematurely.

The plan for manufacturing should specify what portion of the product will be produced internally and how and where the remainder will be outsourced. It should describe the capital investments and facilities required, if any. And it should indicate how costs, inventories, and time to market will be reduced and quality improved over time.

Marketing and sales plans explain how the choices made at Stages 2 and 3 will be carried out. What reliance will be placed on direct or indirect channels? How will marketing communication be handled? What will be done to launch the product effectively? Answer these questions and spell out the sequence of actions.

You should also describe any distinctive aspects of the overall management or administration of the business. For example, if the business is going to rely heavily upon alliances with other suppliers and partners, determine how you will negotiate and manage those agreements along with a timetable.

Activity Schedule

Once the functional elements have been defined, record them in a single comprehensive multi-year schedule with the interrelationships and priorities noted. This schedule ensures that the different business functions will execute their responsibilities in the necessary sequence and that key milestones are identified for overall management purposes. Once the milestones have been defined and agreed upon, failure to meet them should be viewed as a problem indicator and taken as a signal of the need to carefully review progress and institute any necessary changes in plan.

Resource Requirements

The final, and most significant, component of the Business Plan is the identification of the resources required to execute the plan. These fall into three categories: human resources, equipment and facility resources, and financial resources.

Human Resources: Organizational Chart and Job Descriptions

The value chain you defined at the third stage can serve as the basis for outlining the initial organization and defining the kinds of people needed to staff it.

First of all, you will need a President or General Manager with overall responsibility for the business. The heads of each of the essential functions—R&D, Operations, Marketing, Sales, Administration, and Finance—will report to the President. If some of those functions are outsourced, then responsibility for them may be combined with one of the other functions.

Each of those functions will have a staff defined by the nature and extent of the activity as described earlier.

Add a description of each job associated with the key boxes in the Organizational Chart. This will guide the recruitment process at the next stage and can serve as a check that the number of staff is being kept to a minimum while still acquiring the necessary skills.

Equipment and Facility Requirements

Most of the individuals who fill the positions on the organizational chart will require offices or laboratory space, although some may be able, at least initially, to operate from their homes. You will have to decide whether they should all be located together in one place, or whether several geographically distributed spaces can suffice. However, experience suggests that in the early stages of a business, colocation is extremely valuable and should be a high priority.

Consider also the need for manufacturing space, warehousing, customer demonstration facilities, development laboratories, conference rooms, and eating and break facilities. An architect or office or factory planner can help you figure the right space allocations and costs.

Specify any special equipment for manufacturing and laboratories, as well as the general office equipment that is indispensable to modern office functioning. No business can operate without computers, printers, copiers, facsimile machines, networks, and external network access, and many require a variety of new digital tools, such as scanners, document repositories, Internet home page servers, and video or document conferencing facilities.

Financial Plan

Taking all of the above information into account, it is now possible to put together an income statement for several years of the business. The growth model will enable the estimation of revenues. The functional plans and the organizational charts should enable you to estimate cost of goods sold, gross profit, operating expenses and PBT. They should also specify the needs for capital investment and working capital to cover the costs of operation. From that information, you can estimate the cash investment required. You need then to determine how cash needs will be met. What combination of equity and debt best suits the business? With that assumption, the equipment and facility requirements, and rules of thumb about inventories, receivables, and payables, you will be able to create the balance sheet for the first years of the business.

Investors will want to see five years of income statements, balance sheets, and cash flow statements. How fast is the company growing revenues? Is there steady progress toward profitability? How much cash is required to reach positive cash flow? Are the ratios "reasonable" compared to similar companies? How good is the return on sales? Does the net present value, internal rate of return or return on equity meet the requirements of investors? A venture capitalist will want to know what the market value is likely to be at the time of an Initial Public Offering (IPO) and how that translates into an internal rate of return on its investment. And that will depend upon the attractiveness of the market, the growth rate of the company in that market, its perceived competitive position and its prospects for profitability.

Business Plan

You are now in a position to prepare a business plan, which you can use to obtain funds to proceed with the business, to attract participants, and to guide its implementation. Traditional business plans come in a variety of formats. The one presented here contains the same information in a slightly non-traditional order, which is intended to be more consistent with the logic of the six-stage process for taking technology to market.

- Introduction and Overview of Business Concept
- Opportunity Description

○ Markets and Customers

Characterize the target market segments by their specific requirements and sizes over the first few years of operation. Describe the current and anticipated substitutes and competitive offerings.

○ Offerings vs. Competition

Describe the specific products or services that will be offered over the first few years. Compare them to substitutes and competitive offerings.

○ Growth Model

Based on the above, describe the projected numbers of units sold and price levels over the first few years of operation.

• Action Plan
   ○ Functional Plans

   Describe what each function—R&D, Marketing, Operations and Sales—will do to achieve the projected growth.

   ○ Activity Schedule

   Lay out the activities in the functional plans on a single time schedule and show the key milestones that must be met along the way for the plan to be accomplished.

• Resource Requirements
   ○ Organizational Chart and Job Descriptions

   Describe the key functions and staffing requirements needed to carry out the plan.

- ○ Equipment and Facilities Requirements
    Describe the requirements for equipment and facilities to support the business.

- ○ Financial Plan
    Present the projected income statements, balance sheets and cash flow statements for the first three to five years of operation.

- Risk Assessment
    - ○ Evaluation
        Describe and estimate the primary risks and uncertainties in your plan. Include technology and product risks, manufacturing risks, market risks, competitive risks and staffing and implementation risks.

One element that business plans often require is an identification of the key personnel, usually the president and his or her direct reports. In this approach, the identification of those people occurs in the next stage. You may have to wait until you undertake the next step before submitting your business plan to some funders. The outline here would be elaborated to include the education and work experience of the key participants.

VI.

THE BUSINESS START-UP

CHALLENGE
*Establishing the business and
adapting the plan to reality.*

WITH THE BUSINESS PLAN in hand, you can set about creating the business that it describes. To do so, you will have to obtain funding, hire the key functional executives, acquire facilities and equipment, establish the organization, hire the remainder of the staff, negotiate agreements with suppliers and partners, and begin operations.

Obtaining Funds

You face one of two situations. In the first, your technology was developed within an existing company and the objective is to start a new business within that company. In the second, you have developed or acquired technology and your objective is to start a new company. Obtaining funds is obviously different in each case.

Existing Business

If you are working within an existing business and the technology was developed in its laboratories, then the primary source of funding will most likely be the business. You will have to convince the senior management that your business plan satisfies their investment criteria. Businesses vary considerably in the ways in which they balance strategic and financial criteria and how they weigh investments in existing businesses versus those in new businesses. You should by this time have a good sense of the situation within your own company. It is up to you to use that knowledge to shape your business plan appropriately and to convince senior management to fund your business.

Much has been written about the management of new ventures within existing companies. (See Reference 4.) The record is mixed, because the existing business' short-term profit and loss considerations can be applied inappropriately to a start-up in its early stages. You should try to convince senior management to measure your business by cash usage and achievement of milestones, rather than net profit and achievement of annual plans. Nevertheless, you can expect that the financial goals to which you will be held will be those of the larger company. You will be under pressure to satisfy annual goals for profitability rather than for cash usage, milestone achievement and growth.

New Business

If you are independent from any ongoing business and have ownership of the technology underlying your proposed business, then you have a wide range of funding opportunities. You can draw on private equity capital–

your own, your relatives', your friends', wealthy individuals ("angels")—giving up some ownership of the business in exchange for the necessary cash. You can go into personal debt by taking a second mortgage on your house; you can extend your credit cards; you can borrow from friends or relatives. And you can go to professionals who invest regularly in new technology businesses: venture capitalists and some investment bankers.

This is not a book about raising venture capital funds. There is a sufficiency of such books. (See References 8, 9, 14.) However, you should recognize that in exchange for funding, you will be acquiring very interested part-owners, who will want to closely monitor and play a strong role in the key decisions about the business, and whose goal will be to "cash out" subsequent to an IPO, or through sale of your company. These part-owners can be a substantial help, providing advice based on experience with other technology start-ups and links into networks of qualified professionals who may join your business or serve it as consultants or suppliers.

In contrast to the corporate situation, the venture capitalists will look to maximize the market value of your business at the time of the IPO. To that end, they will be most interested in growth and the potential for profitability. They are likely to be willing to forego early profitability in exchange for more growth. However, the resource they monitor is cash. This will be doled out in tranches based on your accomplishment of key milestones. For each infusion of cash, you may have to give up another piece of ownership.

Getting Started

Congratulations are in order once again. When you have reached this stage you have taken your technology idea and expanded it into a fully developed plan for a business. You have also obtained the funding to put the plan into effect. Your task now is to take the plan you have prepared and make it a reality.

To do so, however, you will have to employ new skills. Leadership and operational management skills are distinct from the technological innovation and business planning skills that have been required to this point. If you possess these new skills in the same measure as you do those that have brought you to this point, you are a rare individual indeed. Generally, you will have to call upon others with the requisite skills to join your team.

You will probably even be asked to turn general management responsibility for the business over to an experienced business person. This can be one of the most difficult steps for technologists who have carried their "baby" this far. By now you have a taste of business and believe that the same basic intelligence and determination that brought you to this point can carry you through the business' start-up and operations phases. Sadly, with rare exceptions, intelligence and determination are not sufficient; they must be supplemented by experience. An experienced business person, who has been through the start-up of other companies and seen, and internalized, the challenges that must be faced, brings substantial value to a new business. Much of it is in his or her "fingertip feel" for the requirements of building and running a business.

This is the time to bring on the most important hire that will be made—the business' president or general manager. It is difficult enough to start a new business; it is almost impossible to do so with a president who is learning to be a business manager and leader at the same time.

Establishing the Organization and Hiring

Governance

If you have created an independent business with a corporate form, you will have to set up a board of directors who will have overall responsibility to the shareholders for the operations of the business. In addition to representatives of the principal funders, you will probably want to invite board members whose experience, contacts and personal judgment can assist the senior team to make the business a success. The board will be extremely important both through its formal responsibilities and through its capacity for advice and assistance. Therefore, the selection of a board is one of the most important early tasks in the establishment of a business.

In the case of a business within an existing business, the reporting relationship depends upon the structure and policies of the existing business. Some companies establish separate organizations to incubate new businesses, while others have them report to existing businesses, or to a function, such as research. Because start-ups require intensive attention and should be subject to different performance expectations than mature businesses, they should report to a special function. And because they are profit and loss centers, with unanticipatable swings, they should not be located within cost centers that do not have the resources to cover those variations. An alternative arrangement would be to have responsibility assigned to a board of company executives, who in turn report to the company's president.

Recruitment of the Senior Management

It is now time to put names to the organizational chart that was included in the business plan. Whoever has funded your venture will provide a lot of help in selecting the senior leadership team, especially the president. Venture capitalists usually will not fund a start-up until they know who that team will be. In that case, you can benefit from their advice and connections, as well as those of others in the industry, to help find strong candidates in advance of the funding. If you are in a company, you may be able to draw upon skilled managers from within. However, unless senior management assigns a high priority to your business, and provides direct support, you may not be able to recruit suitable candidates, who are likely to be highly valued and guarded by the existing businesses. In that case, it will be best to seek your senior team outside the company.

Ideally, the candidates should have a successful track record of management in small start-up businesses. Large company experience is helpful, but not as good, because it does not usually provide such intense exposure to all aspects of a business, nor does it develop the strong concern for cash management that must be a hallmark of tightly funded new businesses. Start-ups also require rapid decision-making and swift strategy changes, skills that are not easily learned in a large corporation. This is another reason for recruiting the senior team from outside, even when starting a new business within an existing company.

Two other aspects of experience are important: functional specialty and industry. Your ideal senior management candidates will have had substantial experience in the functional specialty you want them to lead and in an industry as close as possible to the one you are entering. To repeat: you want a team that can start doing its job at high effectiveness from the very first day; no one should be learning his or her job at the same time.

The first hire, ideally, will be the president/general manager. That person will then take the lead in recruiting the senior team, drawing upon contacts in the industry and, as appropriate, recruitment firms that specialize in the particular functional or industry specialty. Although newspaper advertisements may work for lower levels of seniority, it is not the best way to find highly qualified senior management, who may not be actively seeking new employment at the time you are hiring.

No matter how good the team, it will still encounter many issues that require additional specialized knowledge and experience. To help with such issues, it must select good advisors in fields such as accounting, corporate law, intellectual property and public relations. If the business is a part of a larger corporation, the advice is likely to be available through the corporate functions. Venture capitalists can generally help the businesses they support find experienced and capable advisors.

Compensation

Starting a new business is a more than usually risky activity, even when done inside an existing company. Venture capitalists insist that the management of their start-up ventures participate in that risk by taking compensation that depends upon performance, generally through ownership of a portion of the company. In that way, they ensure the dedication, hard work and personal sacrifice that improve the chances for success in a risky venture. We often hear of the managers of new businesses who become extremely wealthy when the business has its IPO. We rarely hear, however, of the many managers who have worked long hours at low salaries for years, without reaching an IPO before the business failed. New business start-up is a real risk that has both an up side and a down side.

The insight of the venture capitalists applies within existing businesses as well. To get the dedication of the senior team, the compensation package should reflect the risk. In exchange for giving up the security offered by the existing business and for a lower base salary level, team members should be placed on a compensation plan that emulates the kinds of returns that start-up managers can receive. Such a plan will also be required to attract experienced start-up management from outside. You can create such a plan in a variety of ways, each of which must be tuned to the specific needs of the business. For example, you can base compensation on shares in a pool formed from a portion of one of the following:

- Increase in market value of the business (as measured by an actual sale or an independent appraiser).

- Cumulative net profit.

- Returns that exceed what the same investment would have produced if it had been invested at the company's cost of capital (the Economic Value Added–EVA).

The payment would be made based on one of these valuations after a pre-specified number of years, such as five to seven.

This risk-dependent compensation is often extended throughout the company in order to encourage common interests and a shared dedication in all employees.

Facilities and Equipment

With money and the senior team on board, you must now locate and prepare the facilities that the new business will require. Much depends upon the specifics of the business. Does it require manufacturing space? Will it hold large inventories? Is access to transportation important? Is the center of the industry in a certain geographic location? Does it need to have sales and support offices close to its customers? Will customers visit the site? Is a demonstration facility required? Are conference rooms important? What about laboratories for product development?

The answers to these questions are so business specific that not much general advice can be given. There are two guidelines, however:

- First, keep costs to a minimum by finding low cost space and minimizing renovations. Save improvements and finer facilities for the time when the business has established itself.

- Second, retain the maximum possible flexibility. Try to find space where growth is possible; and, if necessary, shrinkage. Keep leases as short as you can.

Similar principles apply with respect to furniture and equipment. Keep it simple and inexpensive. Use information technology extensively to reduce the need for support personnel. Even laboratory and manufacturing equipment expenses should be minimized and flexibility retained by leasing instead of purchasing wherever possible and economically reasonable.

Establishing Functions

Now that the funding, senior team and facilities are in place, it is time to begin operations. The first step should be for the senior team to work through the business plan so that they thoroughly understand it and their responsibilities under it. Minor modifications that incorporate the specific knowledge of the team and changing external conditions should be made. If major modifications prove necessary, they should be made as well, but it will be necessary to go back to the funders to inform them of the changes and obtain their agreement. By the end of this process, the business plan should be the senior team's plan, one that they fully understand and are committed to achieving.

The functional leaders will then be responsible for establishing their functions and beginning their operations.

They will have to hire their teams and work out their functional plans.

Work can now begin with the goal of bringing the offering to market as soon as possible.

Establishing Alliances and Partnerships

The final aspect of preparing the business for its launch into the market is the negotiation of the alliances and partnerships required for its success. Some of these may be critical to your success, if they entail, for example, the provision of products that are complementary to yours. The success of the silverless film for the graphic arts industry mentioned earlier depends critically on alliances with the imagesetter manufacturers, who must agree to provide suitably modified imagesetters.

For a new business, you may find it difficult either to attract the attention of desirable partners or to negotiate mutually beneficial agreements. Your situation is certainly better if you are part of an existing business with resources and a reputation than if you are an independent firm. You may also be in a better position if your new offering has a strong prospect of success in an attractive market and your prospective partners' businesses will benefit directly from your success. Failing those advantages, you may be able to use an equity position in your company to attract the active participation of a key partner. This will, obviously, have to be done only after approval of your primary funders.

Despite the difficulties of doing so, building a network of partners and allies may be one of the best ways for a small start-up business to improve its chances of success. Allies and partners provide an access to resources and skills that would be difficult for a start-up to obtain itself. They can help in making contact with customers and suppliers and they can be a source of advice and guidance in entering the market. And, of course, they can carry out the functions that you have decided to outsource.

If alliances and partners are critical to your business success, they should be one of the most important responsibilities of the president/general manager.

Business Reports

As you enter operations, you must supplement the documents that describe what you intend to do with regular written reports of your progress.

Business Plans—Strategic and Annual

The business plan, both in its multiyear strategic form, and its more detailed annual tactical form, will continue to be required for internal management and for communication with funding sources. You can adapt the formats described earlier for the strategic plan. The annual plan will focus on the key goals for the year and the planned budgets.

Monthly Reports

Each function should submit monthly progress reports, covering both financial performance and functional achievements, to internal management. The finance function is responsible for preparing financial reports for

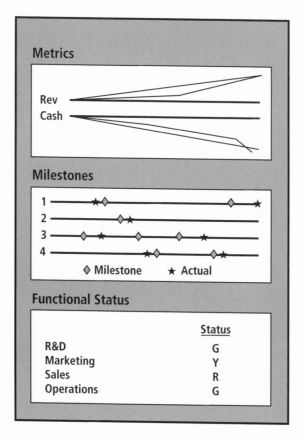

Figure 7. Summary monthly report

the business as a whole. These data can be extracted and used as the basis for a regular monthly report to the board (in the case of an independent start-up) or the responsible senior management (in the case of start-up within an existing business).

For these reports, a three-part summary format may be helpful. The first part should show the actual values of the principal performance metrics plotted month-by-month in comparison to the planned values. The second part should show the planned milestones plotted over time in comparison to the date of actual accomplishment. The third part should show the status of each of the principal functional activities, coded green for on plan, red for off plan and non-recoverable, and yellow for off plan but recoverable. This three-part summary format enables senior management to gain a quick visual appreciation of the state of the business against its goals for the year.

Since new businesses are inherently risky, it is not unusual for internal or external events to force a substantial change in the annual plan during the year. It is essential to retain the flexibility to make such mid-year corrections . . . and to keep the business' funders informed of them.

VII.

MARKET ENTRY

CHALLENGE

*Taking the offering to market and meeting the
ultimate challenge: satisfying real customers in
the face of competition and making a profit
(and sometimes revising the Business Plan
based on hard experience).*

FINALLY, AFTER LONG AND intense effort, your technology is ready to enter the market as an offering designed, produced, marketed and distributed by the company you created for that purpose. Congratulations, once more. But the battle for success is far from over. In a real sense, it has just begun.

While you have been building your business and preparing your offering, the market you are targeting has evolved, other offerings have come to market and your potential customers have placed many other priorities on their agendas. Most likely, no one has been waiting expectantly for your product to be launched. Your challenge then is to capture the attention and the buying decisions of unknowing and possibly indifferent customers and to deliver profitably an offering that satisfies their real requirements.

Now is the time when the marketing function earns its keep. It is also the time when the senior team is likely to be tested by unexpected difficulties in getting the product to market on time, the arrival of unanticipated competition, unforeseen performance problems in the field and issues in matching supply to demand. The business will be melded—or melted—in the hot forge of the marketplace. When it survives the tests, the team will be stronger and more unified.

Marketing Strategy

The key issue for the launch is how to position the offering in the marketplace. This requires answering a set of questions:

- Who are the primary customers and what do they want?

- Who are the competitors and what do they offer?

- What are your offering's distinctive advantages for the primary customers?

- What are the principal messages that should be delivered to the market?

With the answers to those questions, marketing should be able to prepare the advertising, press releases and sales collaterals that will support the launch. In doing so, they may also become engaged in naming the offering and designing its packaging.

Launch

There are many ways to launch a new product or service, and a number of good books cover the subject. (See Reference 11.) The goal is to gain the attention and interest of your potential customers efficiently, covering the target at the lowest cost. Press releases, press conferences, industry journal articles, booths at industry shows, visits to industry analysts and advertising in journals and newspapers are the traditional tools. Many specialist companies exist who will help to orchestrate launches in specific industries. They should be well known to the marketing senior manager.

One approach that is useful in most industries is to pay attention to influencing the influencers. Who are the individuals, journals, newsletters and companies whose opinions your industry listens to? Is there a hierarchy in which certain individuals or publications set the opinions that others adopt? Using the answers to these questions, you should target personal attention to the key influencers well before the launch. Where appropriate, they engage them as consultants to help shape the offering. In most cases, they can be given early notice of the launch under non-disclosure. That will allow them to prepare their own articles or publications for release at the time of launch and enable them to comment to journalists and investment analysts who will call them for their opinions.

As reactions to your launch are published, you should be prepared to amplify the positive reactions in advertising and as reprints for sales collaterals. To the extent possible, you should also deal with the negative

reactions, by preparing counterarguments and by planning
for future upgrades to overcome identified shortcomings.

Market Learning

Once the product is launched, the time for intensive
learning will begin. There are bound to be unexpected
problems and, perhaps, unanticipated successes. The
problems must be addressed quickly and effectively, with
everybody pitching in as required. Aggressively follow up
the successes to exploit the opportunities that they reveal.

Beyond the unexpected, there will be the anticipated
actual experience of customers using the offering to satisfy
their real requirements. This is the time for studying that
experience and incorporating the lessons in the offering
and in the operations of the business. Keeping the feedback loop from market to business short and fast is one
of the best ways to improve your chances of success. It
is difficult to overemphasize the importance of this fast
feedback.

Market Penetration

Your technology has now been brought from an idea to
a reality in the market. The launch, we expect, will have
been a success. So now it is appropriate for us to offer our
final congratulations! You have worked through each of
the six stages; adding new insight and creative ideas at
each one. You have created a promising business and
brought your technology to market as a successful offering. That is a marvelous accomplishment, and one that

has required the skills of many specialists, in areas distinct from technology. As we promised at the beginning, the technology idea with which you began is one part of the large fabric of creative ideas required to generate a profitable business. Without that technology idea, nothing else could have happened; but without the other ideas, it could not have become the source of real value to customers.

It is now time for us to take our leave. Your business will face new and greater challenges as it strives to move from its initial beachhead to a substantial presence in the market. Other books—and the hard-won lessons of the marketplace—can help you to surmount those challenges. We wish you a full measure of success . . . and the time to enjoy it!

Summary and Checklist

To take a promising technology idea from the laboratory to the marketplace, you must pass through six stages, which successively resolve a sequence of critical challenges. Here, in summary form, are the stages, the challenges faced at each one, and a checklist of the questions you should have answered to succeed in meeting each challenge.

STAGE 1.   TECHNOLOGY IDEA

Challenge: *Establishing that the technology is ready, advantaged and protected.*

Is the technology ready?

Is the technology advantaged?

Is the technology protected?

STAGE 2.   BUSINESS PROPOSITION

Challenge: *Defining a realistic business concept and value proposition.*

Is the offering defined?

Are the target market segments identified?

Is the channel of distribution understood?

Are the competitors and substitutes understood?

Are the complementors identified?

Are the key suppliers known?

Is the value net understood?

Has an estimate of customer value been made?

Will the likely pricing enable a profitable business?

STAGE 3.   BUSINESS MODEL

Challenge: *Designing the value chain: which functions will be performed internally and which externally? Establishing a profitable financial model.*

Has the task for each function been defined?

Have the functions to be performed internally and externally been identified?

Has a pro forma financial model been created?

Are the anticipated returns likely to be attractive to investors?

STAGE 4.   BUSINESS PLAN

Challenge: *Describing the business opportunity. Specifying the action plan. Determining the resource requirements and the financial returns.*

Has the business idea been concisely described?

Have the scope and size of the business opportunity been quantified?

Has a detailed action plan for initiating and operating the business been spelled out?

Have the financials—especially the cash requirements—of the business for the first three to five years been computed?

Have the risks been identified?

Do the financials justify the required investment, given the risks?

STAGE 5.   BUSINESS START-UP

Challenge: *Establishing the business and adapting the plan to reality.*

Has funding been obtained?

Has governance been established?

Has senior management been recruited?

Have other required staff been hired?

Is the compensation plan established?

Have the facilities and equipment been obtained?

Have the functions begun operations?

Are critical alliances and partnerships in place?

Has a reporting system been set up?

Stage 6. Market Entry

Challenge: *Taking the offering to market and meeting the ultimate challenge: satisfying real customers in the face of competition and making a profit (and sometimes revising the Business Plan based on hard experience).*

Have the market positioning and strategy been established?

Has the launch been prepared?

Has the launch succeeded?

Is a process of learning from the market in place?

Have plans for penetrating the market been made?

When you have been able to answer each of these questions positively you will have successfully taken your technology from the laboratory to the market. Creativity and hard work have been required to pass through each stage. And they will continue to be required for business success. Congratulations on the progress you've made and good luck in all that lies ahead!

REFERENCES

1. American Electronics Association, *Operating Ratios Survey,* Washington, D.C.: published annually.

2. Baty, Gordon B., *Entrepreneurship for the Nineties,* Englewood Cliffs, N.J.: Prentice Hall, 1990.

3. Bell, C. Gordon, with John E. McNamara, *High-Tech Ventures: The Guide for Entrepreneurial Success,* Reading, Mass.: Addison-Wesley Publishing Company, 1991.

4. Block, Zenas and Ian C. MacMillan, *Corporate Venturing: Creating New Businesses within the Firm,* Boston, Mass.: Harvard Business School Press, 1993.

5a. Brandenburger, Adam M., and Barry J. Nalebuff, "The Right Game: Use Game Theory to Shape Strategy," *Harvard Business Review,* July–August 1995, pp. 57–71.

5b. Brandenburger, Adam M., and Barry J. Nalebuff, *Co-opetition,* New York, N.Y.: Doubleday, 1996.

6. Davidow, William H., *Marketing High Technology: An Insider's View,* New York, N.Y.: The Free Press, 1986.

7. Dun and Bradstreet Business Credit Services, *Industry Norms and Key Business Ratios,* New York: published annually.

8.   Garner, Daniel R., Robert R. Owen, and Robert P. Conway, *The Ernst and Young Guide to Raising Capital,* New York, N.Y.: John Wiley & Sons, 1991.

9.   Gladstone, David, *Venture Capital Handbook: New and Revised,* Englewood Cliffs, N.J.: Prentice Hall, 1988.

10. Higgins, Robert C., *Analysis for Financial Management, Fourth Edition,* Chicago, Il.: Irwin, 1995.

11. McKenna, Regis, *The Regis Touch: New Marketing Strategies for Uncertain Times,* Reading, Mass.: Addison-Wesley Publishing Company, 1985.

12a. Moore, Geoffrey A., *Crossing the Chasm: Marketing and Selling Technology Products to Mainstream Customers,* New York, N.Y.: Harper Business, 1991.

12b. Moore, Geoffrey A., *Inside the Tornado: Marketing Strategies from Silicon Valley's Cutting Edge,* New York, N.Y.: Harper Business, 1995.

13. Porter, Michael E., *Competitive Advantage: Creating and Sustaining Superior Performance,* New York, N.Y.: The Free Press, 1985.

14. Pratt, Stanley E., *How to Raise Venture Capital,* New York, N.Y.: Charles Scribner's Sons, 1982.

15. Robert Morris Associates, *Annual Statement Studies,* Philadelphia: published annually.

FURTHER READING

Aronoff, Craig and John Ward, *Contemporary Entrepreneurs,* Detroit, Mich.: Omnigraphics, Inc., 1992.

Kunze, Robert, *Nothing Ventured,* New York, N.Y.: Harper Collins Publisher, 1990.

Nesheim, John, *High Tech Start-Up,* Saratoga, Cal.: Electronic Trend Publications, 1992.

About the Author

Dr. Levien is currently responsible for Xerox's ten-year business strategy and its technology strategy. For several years he headed a group that took the lead in creating a number of new businesses, incorporating a range of innovative technologies. For seven years prior to that, he was Vice President of Corporate Strategy.

Before joining Xerox, Dr. Levien was the Director of the International Institute for Applied Systems Analysis (IIASA), an international research institute concerned with public policy problems of global or universal scope, located in Laxenburg, Austria. He was awarded the Ehrenkreuz, First Class, in Science and Art by the Austrian government for his leadership of the Institute.

Prior to IIASA, Dr. Levien spent 14 years at The RAND Corporation, where he held senior management positions concerned with analysis of public policy problems and also did some of the early work on relational databases and inference-making.

Dr. Levien holds a doctorate in Applied Mathematics (Computer Science) from Harvard University and was awarded a bachelors degree in Engineering with Highest Honors from Swarthmore College.

Dr. Roger E. Levien, Vice President, Strategy and Innovation, Xerox Corporation, P.O. Box 1600, Stamford, CT 06904